Super-Duper Science

Spectacular Space!

by Annalisa Suid
illustrated by Marilynn G. Barr

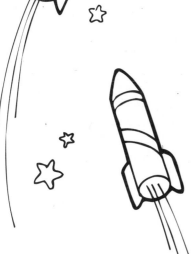

For Dino, Ken, and Paul

Publisher: Roberta Suid
Copy Editor: Carol Whiteley
Design & Production: Santa Monica Press
Cover Art: Mike Artell
Educational Consultant: Tanya Lieberman

Also by the author: *Save the Animals!* (MM 1964), *Love the Earth!* (MM 1965),
Learn to Recycle! (MM 1966), *Sing A Song About Animals* (MM 1987),
and *Preschool Connections* (MM 1993).

On-line address: MMBooks@AOL.com

P.O. Box 1680, Palo Alto, CA 94302

1-878279-90-4

Recycled Paper

Printed in the United States of America

987654321

Contents

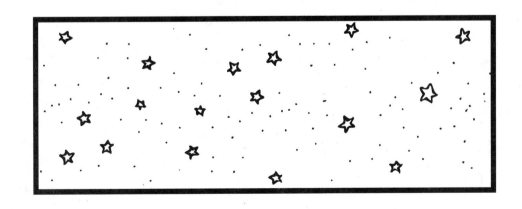

Introduction: Why Space?

Space is spectacular! Your students will learn about the exciting universe while practicing writing, reading, and speaking skills. They'll learn about astronauts, create planetary glossaries, "star" in a musical review, and much more. Most activities may be simplified or extended to suit your students' skill levels.

Spectacular Space! is divided into four parts (plus a resource section). **Hands-On Discoveries** allows children to answer questions they may have, for example, "What are the constellations?" or "How does the moon get 'smaller?'" Reproducible sheets, marked with a special star icon, have directions written specifically for the children.

Nonfiction Book Links features speaking, writing, and reporting activities based on nonfiction resources. Most activities are accompanied by helpful handouts, which will lead children through the research procedure. When research is required, children can look for the facts needed in the library (or in books you've checked out ahead of time). Or they can use the "Super-Duper Fact Cards" located in the resource section at the back of this book. These cards list information for 16 space-related topics. Duplicate the cards onto neon-colored paper, laminate, and cut them out. Keep the cards in a box for children to choose from when doing research. These cards also provide an opportunity for younger children to do research by giving them needed information on simple cards.

The **Fiction Book Links** section uses storybooks to introduce information about interesting space themes, such as stars, the moon, and rockets. This section's activities, projects, and language extensions help children connect with fictional space life. Each "Link" also includes a tongue twister. Challenge children to create their own twisters from the space facts they've learned. Also included in this section are "setting the stage" suggestions for each book.

It's Show Time! presents new songs sung to old tunes, and suggestions for putting on a star-studded production. The songs can be duplicated and given to the children. Write each performer's name on the reproducible program and give copies to your audience.

The first three sections end with a "Super-Duper Project," an activity that uses the information children have learned during the unit. Projects include making a rocketship and giving a tour of the solar system. A performance is a possible "Super-Duper" ending for the "It's Show Time!" section.

All About the Planets

Meet the Planets

Planet Facts:
Our sun is circled by a family of nine planets:

1. Mercury is the closest planet to the sun.
2. Venus is a little smaller than Earth.
3. Earth is the only planet with flowing water and air.
4. Mars is called the "red planet."
5. Jupiter is the biggest planet.
6. Saturn has rings made of icy chunks.
7. Uranus is covered in a thick, blue-green fog.
8. Neptune has eight moons and blue clouds.
9. Pluto is the very smallest planet.

The sun is in the center of this solar system. Earth is the third planet from the sun. Four of the planets are much bigger than Earth.

Everything in the solar system is in motion. Each planet ROTATES or spins. The planets ORBIT (or travel) around the sun. Moons orbit planets.

Our solar system is part of a huge group of stars called the Milky Way galaxy. The Milky Way rotates through the universe.

Creating Constellations

A constellation is a group of bright stars. Long ago, people thought that certain groups of bright stars formed outlines of people, animals, or things in the sky. These groups of stars were given names. Today, astronomers still use these names.

Materials:

"Constellation Patterns" (p. 9), black or dark blue construction paper, white crayons, hole punch (optional), sequins (silver, white, gold, yellow), glue

Directions:

1. Duplicate the "Constellation Patterns" for each child to study.
2. Discuss constellations and ask if any of the children has ever seen one of the constellations in the night sky.
3. Provide black construction paper and white crayons for children to use to either duplicate the constellation patterns or create their own constellations.
4. For added effect, let children decorate the dots of their constellations with sequins.
5. Post the pictures on a "Creative Constellations" bulletin board. These pictures will "twinkle" in your classroom.

Option:

Let children use a hole punch to make holes in their paper to represent the stars. (To punch holes in the middle of the pages, children will need to fold the paper first.) Post these pictures on a window so that the light can shine through.

Constellation Patterns

Orion

Little Dipper

Big Dipper

Cassiopeia

Comet Naming

Halley's comet is the most famous comet of all. It is named for Edmund Halley, an English astronomer who lived over 200 years ago. He was able to predict the year that the comet would reappear. Today, comets are named for the person who spots them first.

Materials:

"My Comet" Hands-on Handout (p. 11), sponges, tempera paint (yellow and white) in tins, black construction paper, scissors, star stickers, silver and gold glitter, glue, marker, index cards

Directions:

1. Duplicate the "My Comet" Hands-on Handout for each child.
2. Discuss the fact that comets are named for the first person who spots them. This means that if any of your students spotted a comet (before anyone else), the comet would be named for him or her!
3. Give each child a chance to be a comet-spotter. Provide tins of tempera paint, round shapes cut from sponges, and black construction paper for children to use to create comets in a night sky. They can drag the sponges horizontally across the pages to create a tail.
4. Provide star stickers, silver and gold glitter, and glue for children to further decorate their pictures.
5. Children can name their comets with their first or last name followed by the word "comet," for example, "Scott's comet," or "Smith's comet."
6. Post the completed comets along with their names (written on index cards) on a bulletin board.

My Comet

What You Need:

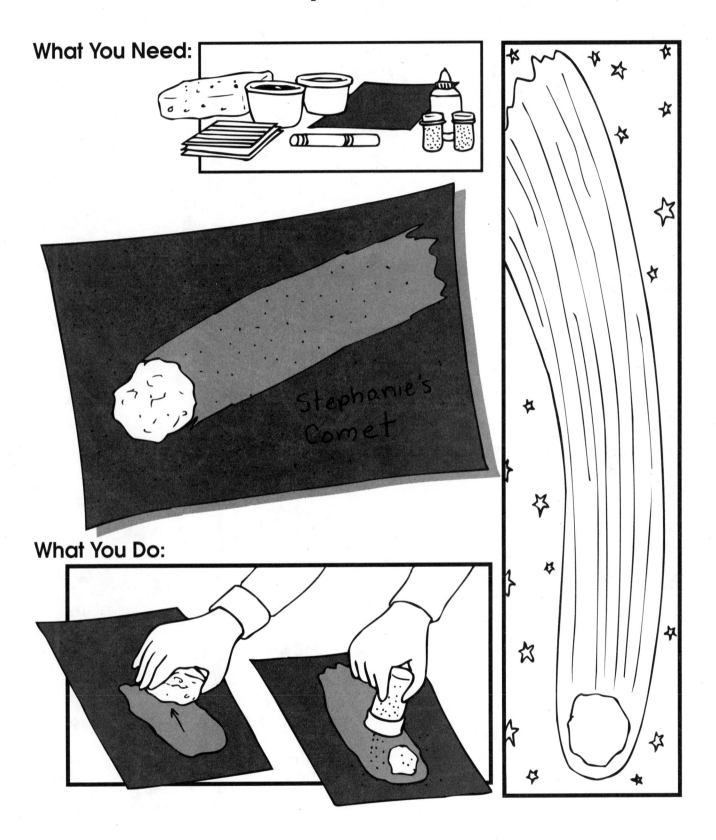

Stephanie's Comet

What You Do:

Earth Speed Sign

Even though Earth circles the sun at about 67,000 miles per hour, we don't feel as if we're moving. But we are! The Earth rotates 365 times—once each day—and travels completely around the sun every year.

Materials:
"Earth Speed Sign Pattern" (p. 13), crayons or markers

Directions:
1. Duplicate the "Earth Speed Sign Pattern" for each child.
2. Discuss the fact that Earth is constantly moving in two ways. It spins, and it also travels around the sun.
3. Explain that Earth moves at approximately 67,000 miles per hour. Have children compare that figure to speeds that they are familiar with: Cars on the freeway travel at 55 miles per hour; people walk at an average of three to four miles per hour; the Apollo spacecraft flew at 25,000 miles per hour.
4. Let the children decorate the Earth speed signs to post around the classroom. These signs will remind the children that they are constantly moving, even when they are standing still!

Earth Speed Sign Pattern

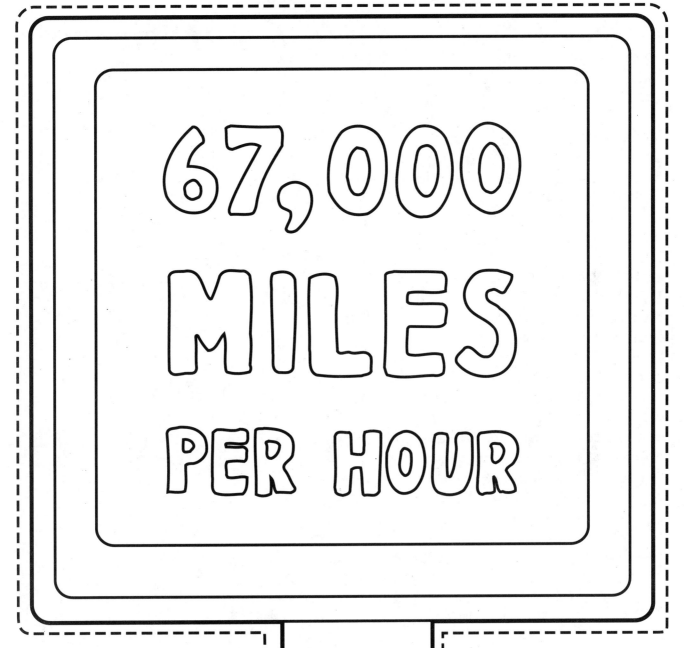

67,000 MILES PER HOUR

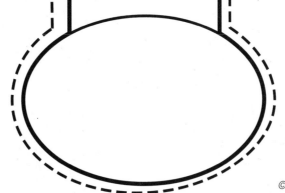

Spinning Earth

Earth spins all the time. While it spins, half is in the light (daytime) and the other half is in the dark (nighttime). The light side spins away from the sun. The dark side spins toward the sun.

Materials:
"Spinning Earth Patterns" (p. 15), heavy paper, brads (two per child), paper plates with hole punched in center (one per child), scissors, 2" x 12" strips of heavy paper (one per child), pencils, crayons, glue, hole punch

Directions:
1. Discuss the fact that Earth spins like a top. The sun is in the center of the Earth's orbit and the Earth spins as it orbits around the sun.
2. Duplicate a copy of the "Spinning Earth Patterns" onto heavy paper for each child.
3. Have children color the sun and one half of the Earth pattern.
4. Have children cut out and glue the sun pattern to the center of a paper plate.
5. Help children punch a hole in each end of their paper strips and show them how to attach the Earth pattern to the heavy paper strip with a brad.
6. Help children attach the other end of the paper strip to the bottom of the paper plate.
7. As children spin the Earth patterns on the brads, have them imagine that the side of the Earth facing away from the sun is dark and the side facing toward the sun is light.

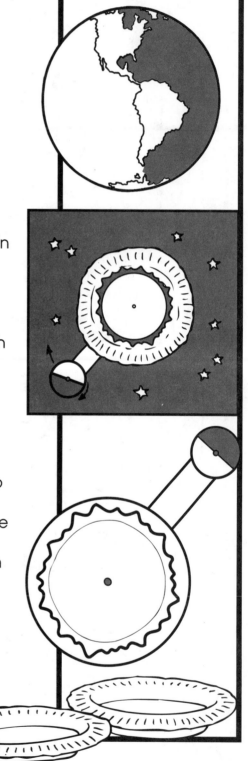

Spinning Earth Patterns

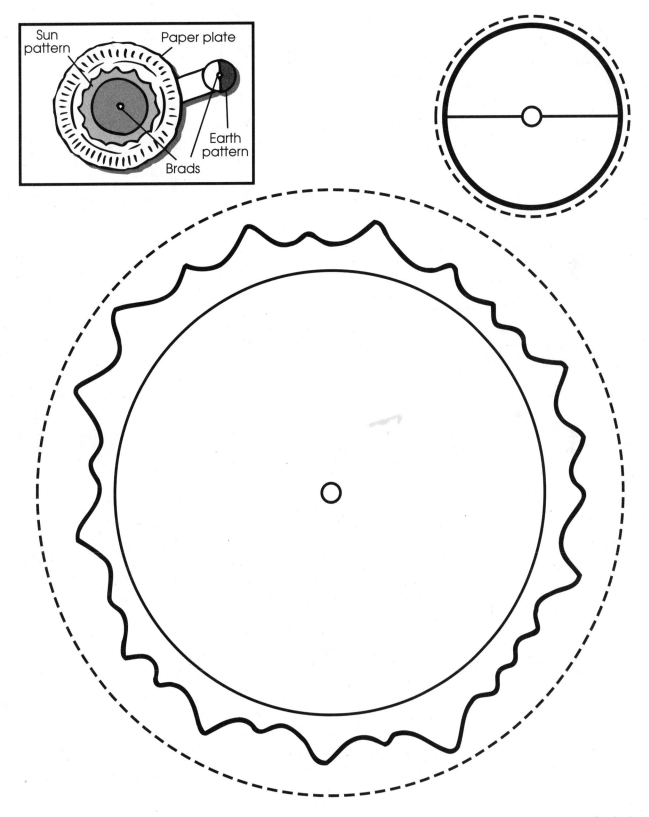

Trip to a Black Hole

Stars are made of hot gases. Eventually the gases cool, and the star collapses. A black hole is a dying star. A black hole has strong gravity. Gravity pulls the gases toward the center. The gases pack closer and closer together. Stars that contain large amounts of gases pack more tightly and become black holes. No light can escape from a black hole.

Materials:

"Trip to a Black Hole" Hands-on Handout (p. 17), Silly Putty (see recipe below)

Directions:

1. Duplicate the "Trip to a Black Hole" Hands-on Handout for each child to study.
2. Provide a ball of Silly Putty for each child to use during the activity. The Silly Putty will represent each child.
3. Lead the children through the steps on the handout.

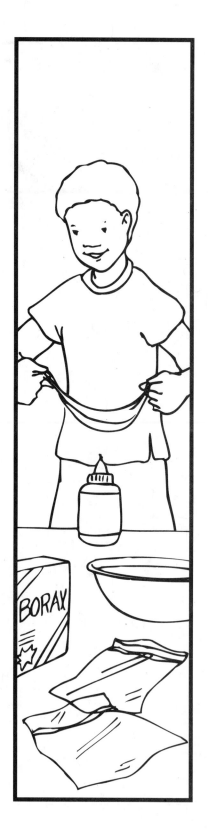

Silly Putty Recipe

Materials:

White glue, water, food coloring (or liquid watercolor), borax, plastic bags with zip seals

Directions:

1. Mix 2 cups white school glue and 1 1/2 cups water.
2. Add food coloring to make a desired shade.
3. In a separate bowl, mix 1 cup water with 3 tsp. borax.
4. Add a little of the borax solution at a time to the glue solution. Stir while continuing to slowly add the borax mixture.
5. Store in plastic bags with zip seals.

Trip to a Black Hole

A black hole is a dying star. This is what a black hole looks like.

(NOTHING! You can't see a black hole.)

1. Imagine that you are traveling through space to a black hole. Feel the gravity pulling you toward it.
(Stretch the Silly Putty.)
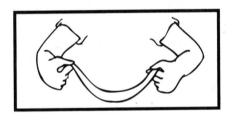

2. The closer you get to the black hole, the longer your body is stretched.
(Stretch the Silly Putty further.)
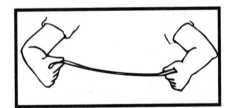

3. You become thinner and thinner.
(Keep stretching the Silly Putty.)
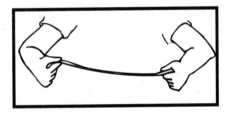

4. Now you are very long and very thin. You move faster and faster toward the black hole. Once you reach the black hole, the gravity is stronger than you can imagine. The gravity now pulls you apart.
(Stretch the Silly Putty until it breaks.)

Weighing in on the Moon

Gravity is a force that pulls things to each other. Gravity makes us come back to the ground when we jump up. The moon has one-sixth the gravity of Earth. This means that an object weighing 60 pounds on Earth would weigh only 10 pounds on the moon. People weigh less on the moon and are able to do more.

Materials:
"Moon Weight" Hands-on Handout (p. 19), scale, pencils, a variety of objects of different weights, ball, yardstick (or tape measure)

Directions:
1. Duplicate the "Moon Weight" Hands-on Handout for each student.
2. Discuss the facts listed above with your students. Make sure that they understand that the less gravity there is, the less they weigh.
3. Have children weigh themselves on a classroom scale. They can do this with a partner: one child steps on the scale and the other notes the weight.
4. Help children divide their weight using the formula on the chart. You can further explain this by showing children objects that would weigh approximately what they would weigh on the moon. For example, if a child weighs 60 pounds on Earth, he or she would weigh 10 pounds on the moon. Show children an object that weighs 10 pounds (or a 10-pound barbell). Tell them that this is how heavy they would be on the moon.
5. Work through the other problems on the page with the students.

Moon Weight

My name is: _____

1. On Earth I weigh: _____

On the moon, I would weigh:

_____ ÷ _____6_____ = _____

(Earth weight)   (my weight)

2. On Earth, I can jump: _____

(how far)

On the moon, I would be able to jump
6 times further than I could on Earth.

_____ x _____6_____ = _____

(Earth jump)   (moon jump)

3. On Earth, I can throw a ball: _____

(how far)

On the moon, I would be able to throw the
ball 6 times further than I can on Earth. On
the moon, I could throw the ball:

_____ x _____6_____ = _____

(Earth throw)   (moon throw)

Watercolor Aurorae

Explosions of energy on the sun's surface can blast out tiny particles that enter Earth's atmosphere and create amazing light displays. These blasts are also called solar flares. On Earth, solar flares can produce the glowing, luminous lights called aurorae that sometimes appear in the night sky. The aurora borealis (northern lights) are visible at the Arctic Circle, and the aurora australis are visible at the Antarctic Circle.

Materials:

Watercolors, paintbrushes, painting paper, photograph books on aurorae (see "Nonfiction Resources," p. 79)

Directions:

1. Describe the northern and southern lights to your students. Aurorae can be many colors, including red, green, blue, and purple.
2. Show aurorae pictures from nonfiction books. If any of your students has seen aurorae, let that child describe the image.
3. Provide watercolors and painting materials for children to create their own aurorae.
4. Post the completed pictures on an "Amazing Aurorae" bulletin board.

Option 1:

If glow-in-the-dark paint is available, let children use this to create their luminous paintings.

Option 2:

Have children work together to paint a cooperative mural. Hang this high on a wall, or post it on the ceiling.

Marvelous Moon Rocks

The moon has no atmosphere and no weather. This means that dust and rocks have stayed in the same positions on the moon for millions of years. The youngest moon rock that scientists have analyzed was 3.1 billion years old. One sample of moon rock taken from the first moon landing was about 4.6 billion years old. This is approximately the same age as Earth.

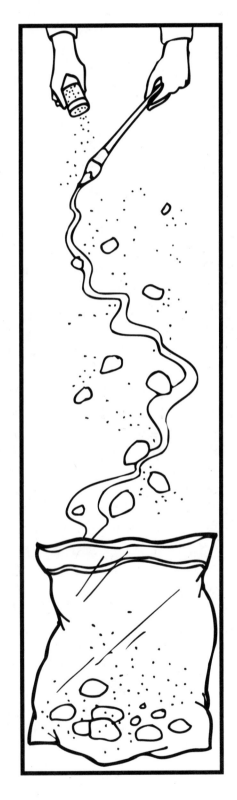

Materials:

Small rocks or pebbles, glue, brushes, multicolored glitter, self-sealing plastic bags, index cards, markers, newsprint

Directions:

1. Discuss moon rocks with your students.
2. Spread newsprint over the work area.
3. Let your children create moon rocks by coating small rocks or pebbles with glue, placing the rocks in a self-sealing plastic bag filled with glitter, and then shaking the bag to coat the rocks. Once the rocks are coated, children can remove them from the bags and shake off the excess glitter over the newsprint.
4. Let the rocks dry.
5. Have your students decide how old their moon rocks are. They should label the age of the rocks on index cards and then glue their rocks to the index cards.
6. Display the completed moon rocks on a "Marvelous Moon Rocks" table.

Option:

Spray-paint rocks with gold or silver paint. (Do this ahead of time.) Children can use these rocks to complete the activity.

Note:

To give your children some concept of how big a billion is, tell them that a billion $1 bills would span the Earth four times around the equator.

Making a Rocket

This journey-to-the-moon activity can be done very quietly, because there is no air on the moon to carry sound!

Materials:
"Rocket Patterns" (p. 23), rocket books (see "Nonfiction Resources"), refrigerator box, tempera paint, paintbrushes, aluminum foil, clear cellophane (for windows), red and orange cellophane (for flames), scissors, tape, glue, stapler, recyclable items (lids, canisters, assorted cardboard boxes), construction paper, markers or crayons, "Marvelous Moon Rocks" display (see p. 21), "Creative Constellations" display (see p. 8)

Directions:
1. Duplicate the "Rocket Patterns" for each child to study. You can also show children pictures of rocket ships.
2. Let children work together to create a rocket. They can use a refrigerator box (or other large cardboard box), tempera paint, aluminum foil, and assorted materials to make their rocket. Red and orange cellophane can be attached to the rear of the rocket to simulate flames as the rocket blasts off!
3. Have children make classroom flags from construction paper and markers or crayons. They can post these flags when they reach the moon. (The astronauts put up a U.S. flag when they landed. They had to stiffen it with wire because there is no wind on the moon.)
4. Children can take turns riding in the rocket.
5. When they reach the moon, they can go on moon walks, pretending to be lighter than they are on Earth. They can even wear "oxygen tanks" (backpacks). Children can visit the moon rock and constellation displays. (On the first moon walk, astronauts collected samples of dust and rock.)

©1996 Monday Morning Books, Inc.

Rocket Patterns

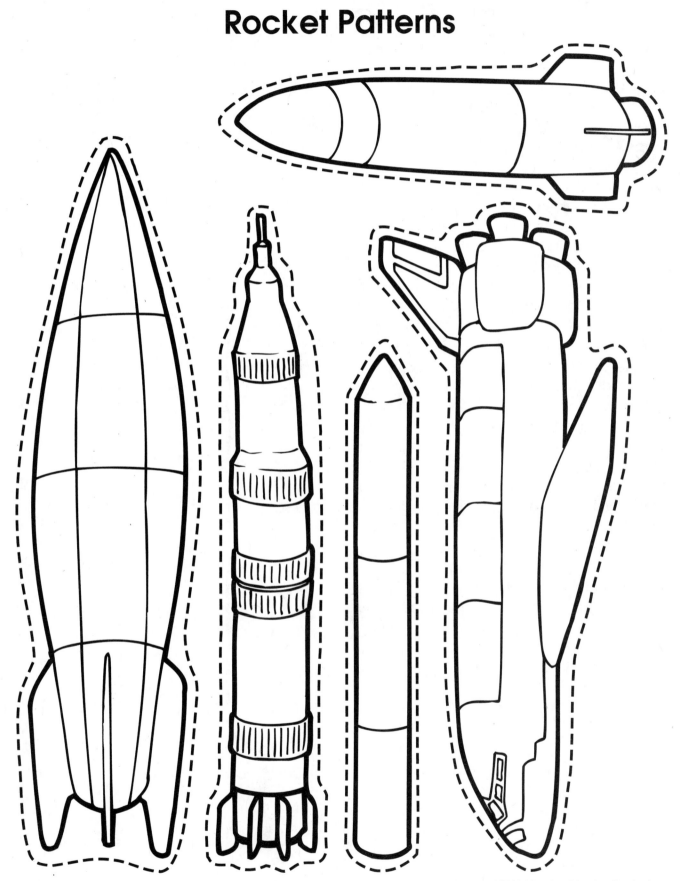

Space Glossaries

Materials:

"Space Glossary" Hands-on Handouts (pp. 25-26), writing paper, pens or pencils, dictionaries, construction paper, stapler, scissors

Directions:

1. Duplicate the "Space Glossary" Hands-on Handouts for each child. Explain that a glossary is a list of special words on a subject with definitions.
2. Have children look up each word in the dictionary.
3. Children should write the definition next to the word to create their own glossaries. Younger children can draw pictures.
4. As children learn new space-related words (or phrases), have them add these words to their glossaries.
5. Provide construction paper and a stapler for children to use to bind their pages together. They can decorate the cover of the book with planetary cutouts.

Note:

For additional words to add to the glossaries, refer to the "Space A to Z List" (p. 78).

Option:

White-out the words on the glossary patterns to make blank pages. Children can use these to write in their own words.

Space Glossary

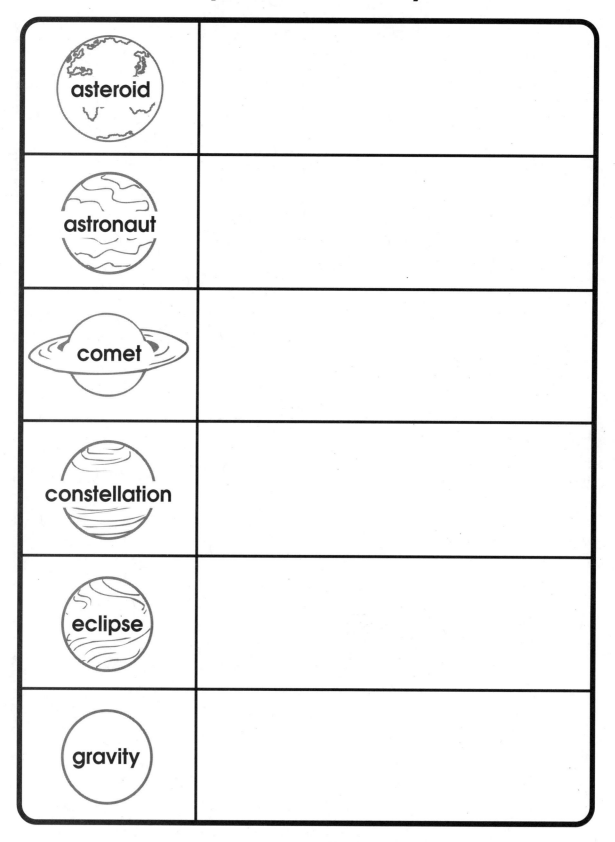

Space Glossary

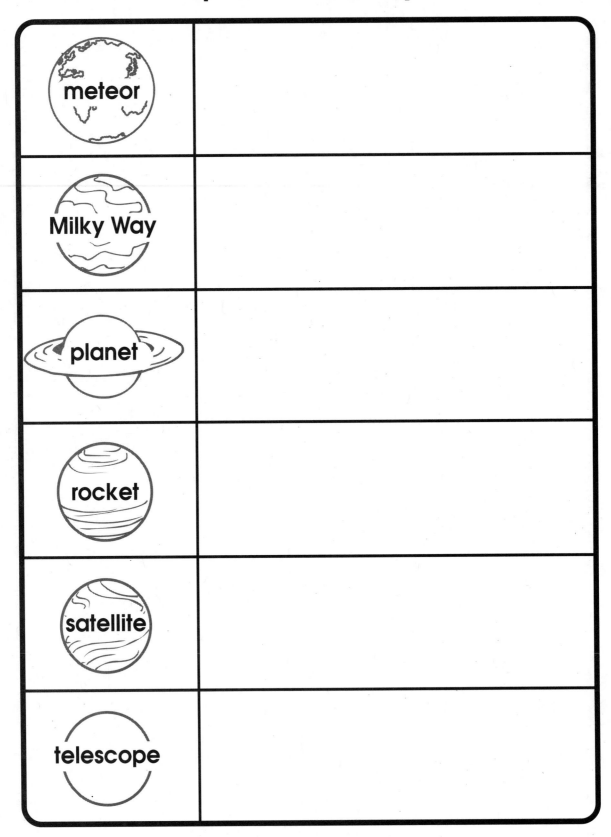

Spelling in Space

Materials:
"Spelling Star Patterns" (pp. 28-29), "Moon Pattern"
(p. 30), scissors, crayons or markers, tape or glue

Directions:
1. Duplicate the "Spelling Star Patterns," making one
sheet for each child and a few extra sheets for teacher
use.
2. Enlarge and duplicate the "Moon Pattern," color,
and post on the bulletin board. Cut out one extra set of
"stars" and post them around the moon.
3. Have children learn how to spell each word.
4. Host a "Spelling in Space" contest in your classroom.
Keep one set of "stars" in a hat and pull out one at a
time, asking each child in turn to spell the word on the
pattern.
5. By process of elimination, continue with the spelling
contest. (Children who misspell a word sit down. The
rest continue to try to spell the words.)

Note:
For additional spelling words, refer to the "Space A to Z
List" (p. 78).

Option 1:
Duplicate blank spelling "stars" and let children write in
their own space-related words.

Option 2:
Duplicate both the moon pattern and "stars" for
younger children. They can simply tape the "stars" to
the moon and practice tracing the words.

Spelling Star Patterns

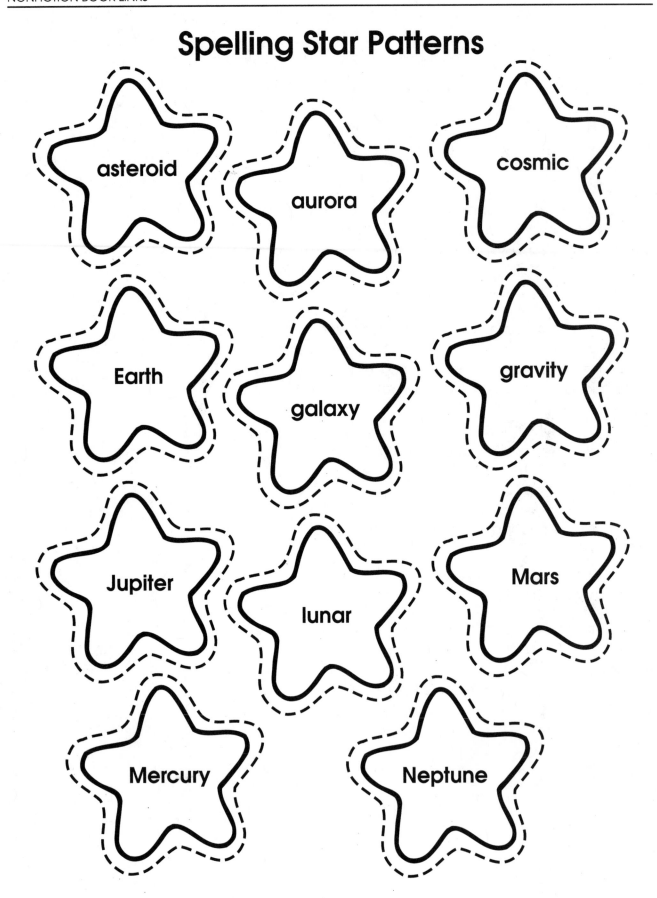

Spelling Star Patterns

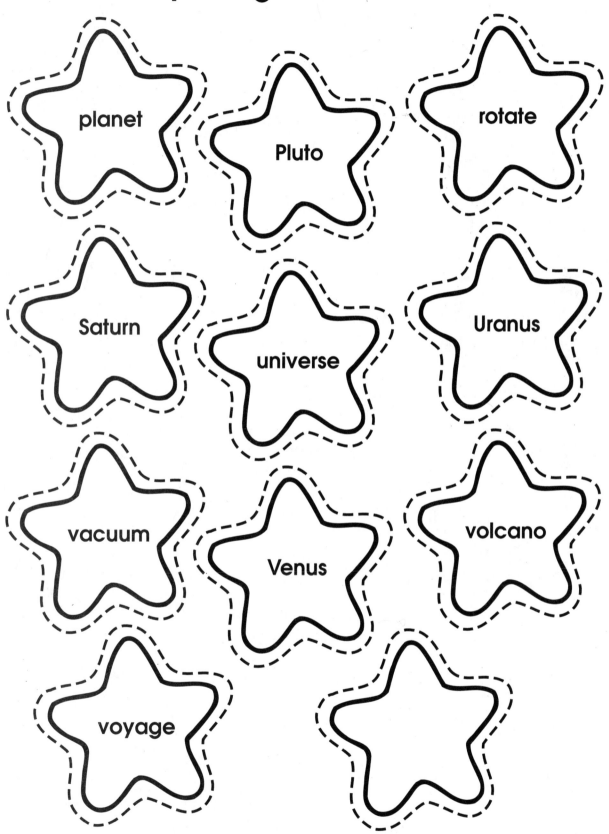

planet

Pluto

rotate

Saturn

universe

Uranus

vacuum

Venus

volcano

voyage

Moon Pattern

Star Fact Chains

Stars give off heat and light because of their hot gases. These gases are what make the stars shine. Stars are so far away from Earth that their distances are measured in light-years, not miles. The sun is eight light-minutes from us. The next star is four light-years away. Some stars are billions of light-years away! Stars look like they twinkle because of how starlight travels through the air around Earth.

Materials:

"Star Patterns" (p. 32), "Super-Duper Fact Card" on stars (p. 75), oaktag or tag board (file folders work well, too), scissors, hole punch, silver or white yarn (or paper clips), pencils or markers, silver glitter, glue

Directions:

1. Duplicate and enlarge the "Star Patterns" onto oaktag or tag board, making at least one star for each child.
2. Have the children cut out the patterns.
3. Let children choose facts to write on their star patterns from the "Super-Duper Fact Card" on stars, or from library books (see "Nonfiction Resources" for suggestions).
4. Children should write their favorite fact about stars on their star pattern.
5. Children can decorate the rims of their stars using silver glitter and glue. Let dry.
6. Show children how to punch a hole in the patterns and string them together to make a chain, using either yarn or paper clips.
7. Hang the chain as a border along a bulletin board.

Option:

Post the completed star facts on a bulletin board in a simple constellation shape, the Big Dipper, for example.

Star Patterns

Where Were You on July 20, 1969?

Almost anyone who was at least 10 years old on July 20, 1969, remembers the moment when astronauts first reached the moon. This report allows students the opportunity to interview real people about this important event.

Materials:

"Moon Landing Interview Sheet" Hands-on Handout (p. 34), "Newspaper Article" Hands-on Handout (p. 35), pencils, books from "Nonfiction Resources" about the event

Directions:

1. Discuss the moon landing with your students. If you watched it on television, describe your feelings. Otherwise, show books (from "Nonfiction Resources") with photographs of the landing.
2. Duplicate the "Moon Landing Interview Sheet" and "Newspaper Article" for each child.
3. Have the children interview their parents, grandparents, or neighbors to find the information they need. If this is not possible, invite a guest speaker (who witnessed the televised reports of the event) to the classroom for the children to interview as a group.
4. Once the children have completed their interviews, have them record their information as articles using the newspaper handouts as guidelines.
5. Bind the completed reports into a classroom paper.

Moon Landing Interview Sheet

Interview someone who remembers the first moon landing. Write your answers under the questions. Write your own question for question 5.

Name of person interviewed: _____

Age of person interviewed: _____

Question 1: Where were you on July 20, 1969?

_____

_____

Question 2: What do you remember about the moon landing? _____

_____

Question 3: How did you feel when Neil Armstrong put up the U.S. flag? _____

_____

_____

Question 4: Would you like to go to the moon? Why or why not? _____

_____

_____

Question 5: _____

_____

Newspaper Article

Use the answers from your Moon Landing Interview to write a short article. Tell the name of the person you interviewed, and how old he or she was on the day of the moon landing. You can use quotes (actual things the person said) in your story. Write a headline title for your newspaper article in the space below.

Planet Placement Mnemonics

Explain that mnemonics are formulas or techniques used to help people remember things. Sometimes they are used to remember spelling rules ("i before e, except after c"), sometimes they are used to remember directions or people's names. Children can make up their own mnemonics to remember the placement of the planets.

Materials:

"Planet Mnemonics" Hands-on Handout (p. 37), pencils, crayons or markers, books on planets from "Nonfiction Resources"

Directions:

1. Duplicate a copy of the "Planet Mnemonics" Hands-on Handout for each child to study. Children can also look at pictures of the planets in the nonfiction books.
2. Let children color in the planets with the crayons or markers.
3. Have the children make note of the order of the planets. Then, on the space below the planet pictures, children can write their own mnemonics for memorizing the order of the planets.

Note:

You can also do this activity as a class, writing the suggestions on the board and then voting for the classroom mnemonic.

Planet Mnemonics

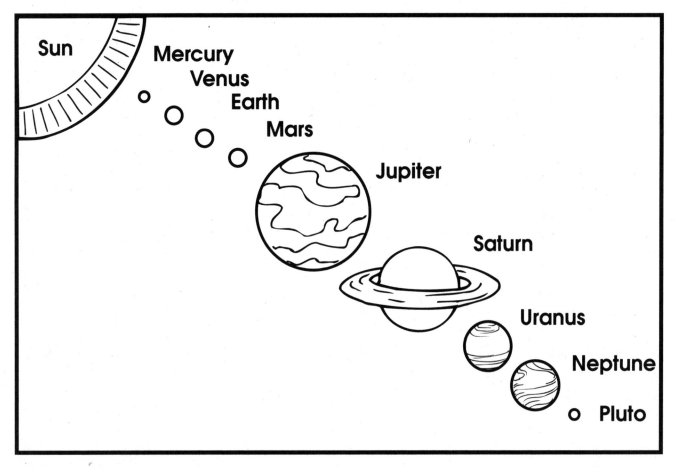

Sun Mercury Venus Earth Mars Jupiter Saturn Uranus Neptune Pluto

This is the order of the planets from the one closest to the sun to the one farthest away.

Write a mnemonic to help you remember the order of the planets.

Mnemonic Example:
My **v**ery **e**xciting **m**other **j**ust **s**at **u**nder **N**ancy's **p**oster.

My mnemonic: _____

_____

_____

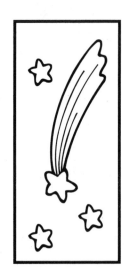

Planet Mobile Report

Materials:
"Planet Mobile Patterns" (pp. 39-42), "Super-Duper Fact Cards" about planets (pp. 70-77), crayons or markers, scissors, pencils, yarn, hole punch, hangers, construction paper

Directions:
1. Divide students into groups of nine. Each child should choose one of the nine planets to research. (Encourage children to choose different planets than the ones they report on for the "Interview with a Planet" activity.)
2. Duplicate and enlarge the "Super-Duper Fact Cards" about planets for children to use to do research. (They can also use books about planets from the "Nonfiction Resources" section.)
3. Duplicate and enlarge one set of "Planet Mobile Patterns" for each group.
4. Let children choose one or two facts about their planets. Have them write the facts on the backs of the planets.
5. Provide assorted markers and crayons for children to use to decorate the front of the planet patterns.
6. Provide construction paper for children to use to cover the body of the hangers.
7. Show children how to punch one hole in each pattern, thread through with yarn, and attach to a hanger. Make sure that children hang the planets in the correct order. (They can refer to "Planet Placement Mnemonics" in order to remember.)
8. Hang the mobile reports in the classroom. Make sure that both sides of the mobiles can be seen—the decorated side and the factual side.

Option:
Invite other classes in to observe the planet mobiles.

Note:
The "Planet Mobile Patterns" are not to scale.

Planet Mobile Patterns

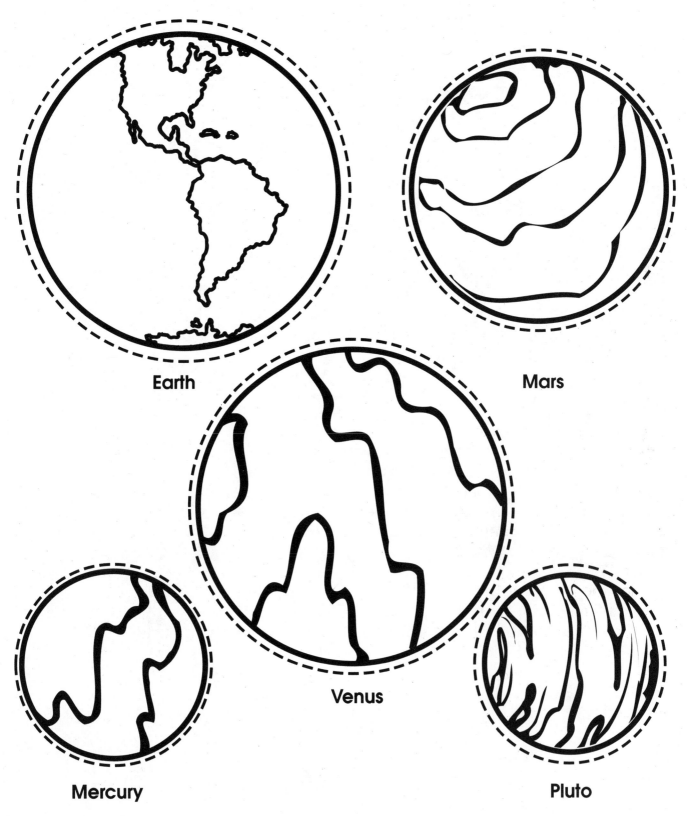

Earth

Mars

Venus

Mercury

Pluto

Planet Mobile Patterns

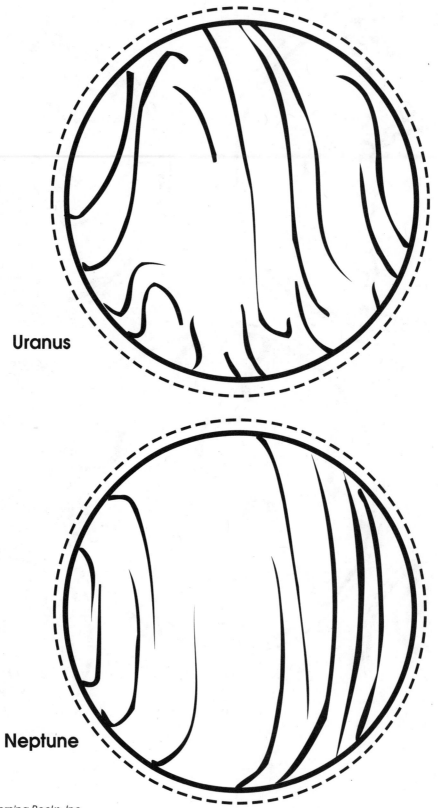

Uranus

Neptune

Planet Mobile Patterns

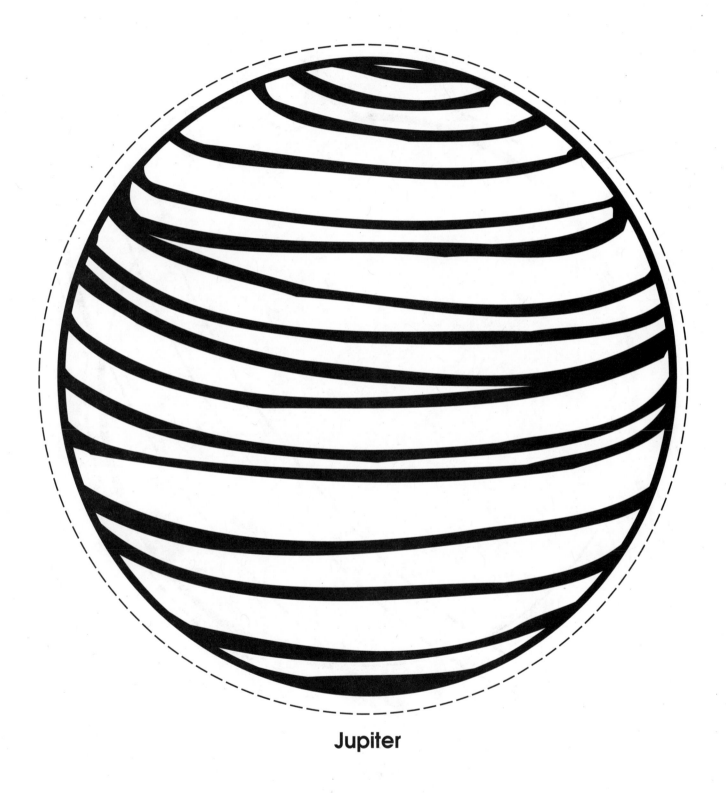

Jupiter

Planet Mobile Patterns

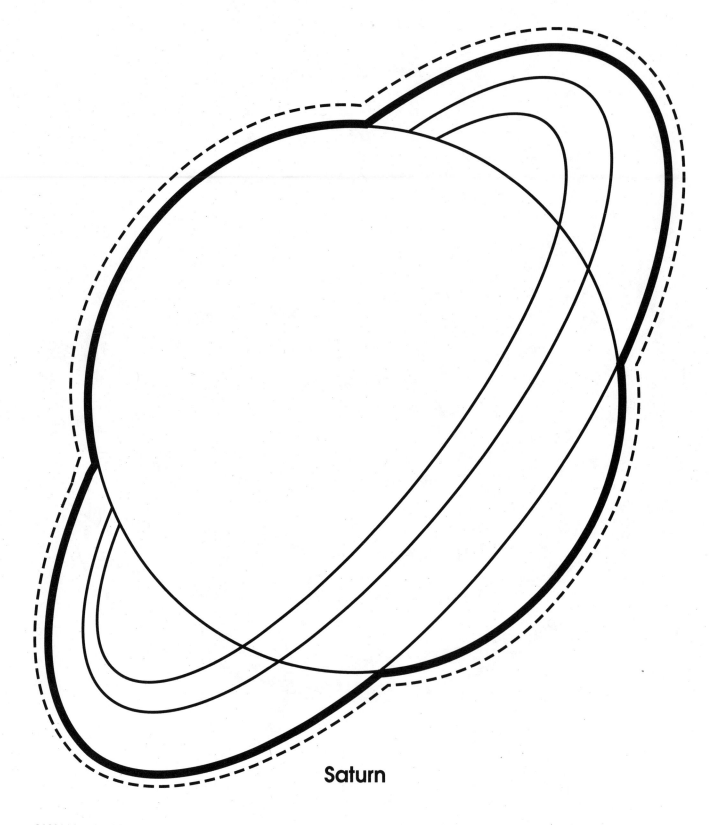

Saturn

Interview with a Planet

Materials:

"Super-Duper Fact Cards" (pp. 70-77), "Planet Fact Sheet" Hands-on Handout (p. 44), "Planet Interview Sheet" Hands-on Handout (p. 45), pencils or markers

Directions:

1. In these reports, children research planets and then play the part of those planets in interview settings.
2. Let each child choose a planet from the "Super-Duper Fact Cards." Children can use the Fact Cards to research their topics. Or they can use books from the library.
3. Duplicate one copy of the "Planet Fact Sheet" hand-out and the "Planet Interview Sheet" for each child.
4. Have the children research their chosen planet using the guidelines on the "Planet Fact Sheet" handout. Then have them write questions based on the facts using the "Planet Interview Sheet" handout.
5. Once the children have finished their research, divide them into pairs. Have each partner take a turn interviewing the other in front of the class.
6. Set up an interview schedule, perhaps working through five to six interviews per day.

Note:

Children can also write reports on other space-related topics. Have them choose from the "Space A to Z List" (p. 78).

Option:

Interviewers can hold simple microphones (cardboard tubes with egg carton sections glued to the top).

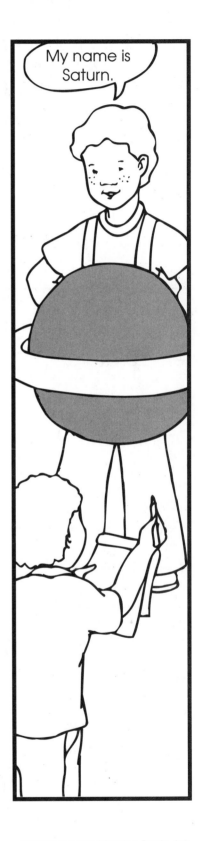

Planet Fact Sheet

Use the fact sheet to record facts about your planet. (Remember to list the books you used.) You can use the back of this sheet if you need more room.

My name is: _____

My planet is: _____

Location (in relation to the sun): _____

_____

Size: _____

Temperature: _____

Moons (how many?): _____

Other facts:

_____

_____

_____

_____

Books I used:

Title: _____

Author: _____

Title: _____

Author: _____

Planet Interview Sheet

Write the answers under the questions. Write your own question for question 5. Your partner will use these questions to interview you in front of the class.

Question 1: What are you called?

_____

_____

Question 2: Where are you located?

_____

_____

Question 3: Is your temperature hot or cold?

_____

_____

Question 4: Can people live on you?

_____

_____

Question 5:

_____

_____

_____

Essay Contest

Students will use the information they've learned in this unit (as well as the reports and crafts) to create a star-studded museum. They can also enter an essay and poster contest.

Materials:
Writing paper, art paper, pencils, crayons or markers, tempera paint, paintbrushes, "Super-Duper Fact Cards" on planets (pp. 70-77), "Award Patterns" (p. 47)

Directions:
1. Provide writing materials and art materials for students to use to design posters and write accompanying essays to answer the questions "What is my favorite planet?" and "Why?" Children can use the information they've researched from their "Interview with a Planet" or "Planet Mobile Reports" to answer these questions. They can also refer to the "Super-Duper Fact Cards."
2. Display the posters and essays at your museum (see p. 50).
3. Duplicate and cut out the "Award Patterns." Give an award to each entry, for example, Most Colorful, Most Imaginative, Funniest, Most Serious, and so on.

Option:
Provide glow-in-the-dark paint for an interesting effect.

What is my favorite planet?

Award Patterns

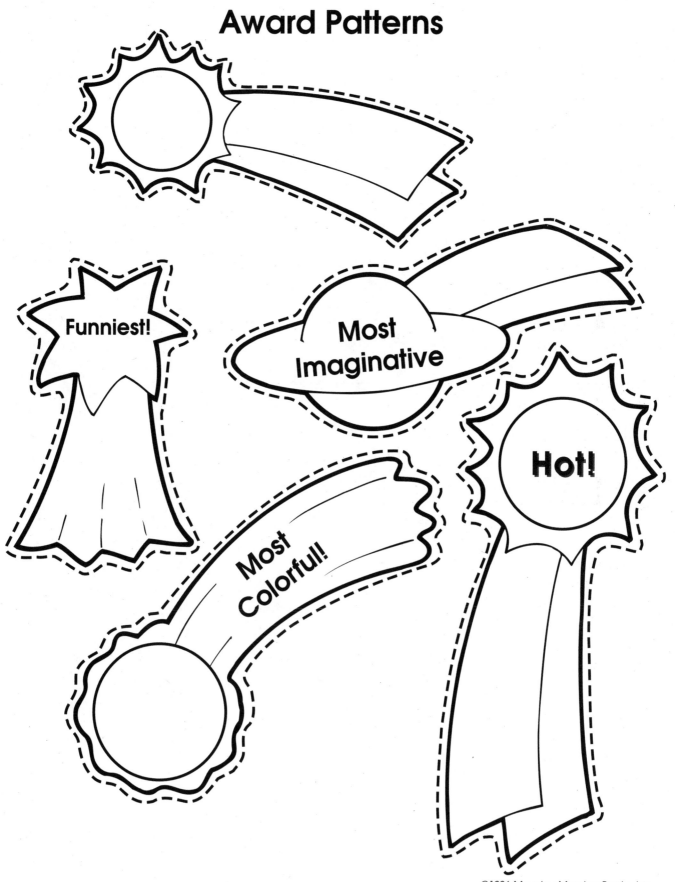

Funniest!

Most Imaginative

Hot!

Most Colorful!

Museum Brochures

Materials:

"Museum Brochure" Hands-on Handout (p. 49), crayons or markers, "Super-Duper Fact Cards" (pp. 70-77)

Directions:

1. Duplicate a copy of the "Museum Brochure" Hands-on Handout for each student.

2. Provide children with crayons or markers to use to design the brochures for the "Tour of the Planets" museum (p. 50). The brochures should be about the topics your students have studied in the "Nonfiction Book Links" unit: stars, planet order, planet descriptions, moon landing, and so on.

3. Children can include pictures and descriptions of the exhibits by coloring and then writing one or two facts about each item. They can use the "Super-Duper Fact Cards" for additional research.

Option:

Include projects from the "Hands-on Discoveries" unit, as well.

Museum Brochure

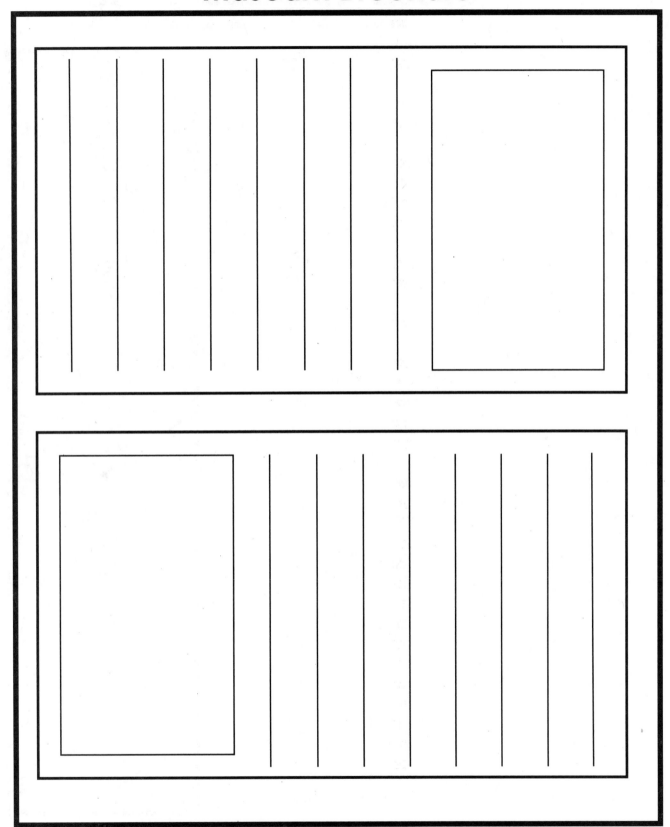

Tour of the Planets Museum

Your students can show off their planetary knowledge in a living museum!

Materials:

Projects from previous activities ("Star Fact Chains," "Planet Mobile Reports," "Space Glossaries," "Museum Brochures," and so on), "Name Tag Patterns" (p. 51), schedule of classes coming to view museum, rope, masking tape, poster board, crayons and markers, paper

Directions:

Several days before:

- Have students make and post posters around the school that promote your museum.
- Invite other teachers to visit with their classes.
- Have students make and distribute invitations for parents and other family members and school administrators.
- Designate museum-visit roles: greeters, docents, museum security, ushers. Use the name tags (p. 51).
- Have students design a floor plan for the museum.

The day before or the day of the museum opening:

- Assemble the museum exhibits: "Essay Contest" entries, "Star Fact Chains," "Planet Mobile Reports," and others.
- Rope off areas that shouldn't be touched.
- Put a masking tape dotted path on the floor.
- Put out the museum brochures for visitors.

The day of the museum opening:

- Bring visitors through your museum.
- Award essays and posters. Assign student docents for each visitor, or have children posted at stations to explain the exhibits.
- Have children give brief reports on the planets based on their "Interview with a Planet" performances.

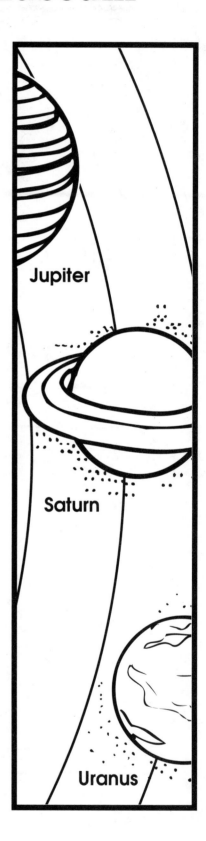

Jupiter

Saturn

Uranus

Name Tag Patterns

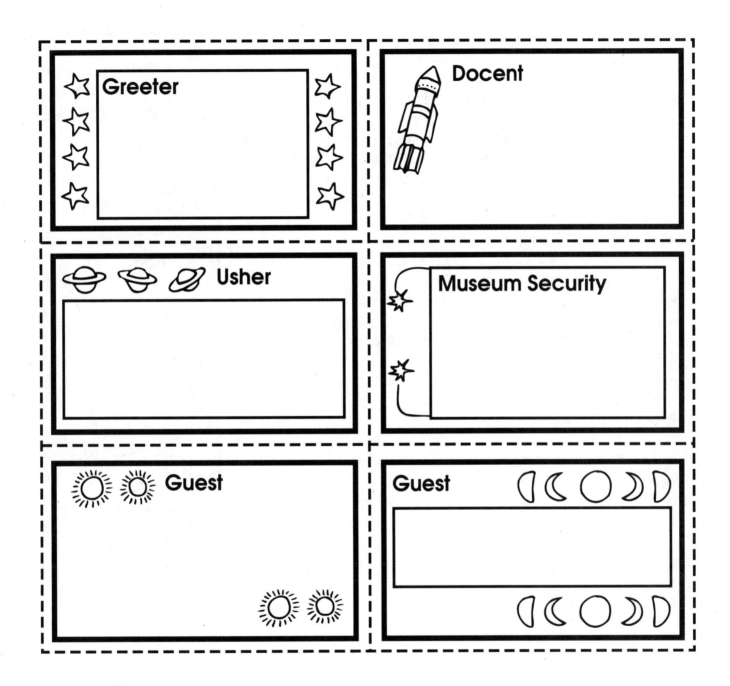

Postcards from Pluto

Story:

Postcards from Pluto by Loreen Leedy (Holiday House, 1993).

This is a factual book presented in an easy-to-read, fictional manner. A group of children go on an imaginary trip through the solar system, writing postcards back home from each planet. Some of the postcards have riddles and poems about the planets.

Setting the Stage:

- Enlarge and duplicate the planetary patterns (pp. 39-42), color, cut out, and post around the classroom.
- Bring in postcards of places around the country (or world) for children to look at. (These cards might give them some ideas for designing their own cards.)
- Write the children's planetary mnemonics (see pp. 36-37) on large pieces of paper and post around the classroom.

Tricky Tongue Twister:

Rings of Saturn spin so swiftly.

Postcards to Earth

Materials:
Postcard-sized pieces of paper (or index cards), crayons or markers, "Planet Stamp Patterns" (p. 54), paste or glue

Directions:
1. Have the children imagine that they are space travelers visiting other planets.
2. Provide postcard-sized pieces of paper and crayons or markers for children to use to create "space" scenes on one side of the cards.
3. The children can write short messages on the backs of the cards. The messages should be about their trip to the other planets, what they have seen, what the weather is like, and so on.
4. Children can address their cards to friends in the classroom.
5. Duplicate the "Planet Stamp Patterns" for children to paste or glue to their postcards.
6. Create an interplanetary message board (on a bulletin board) and post the cards where children can read them.

Planet Stamp Patterns

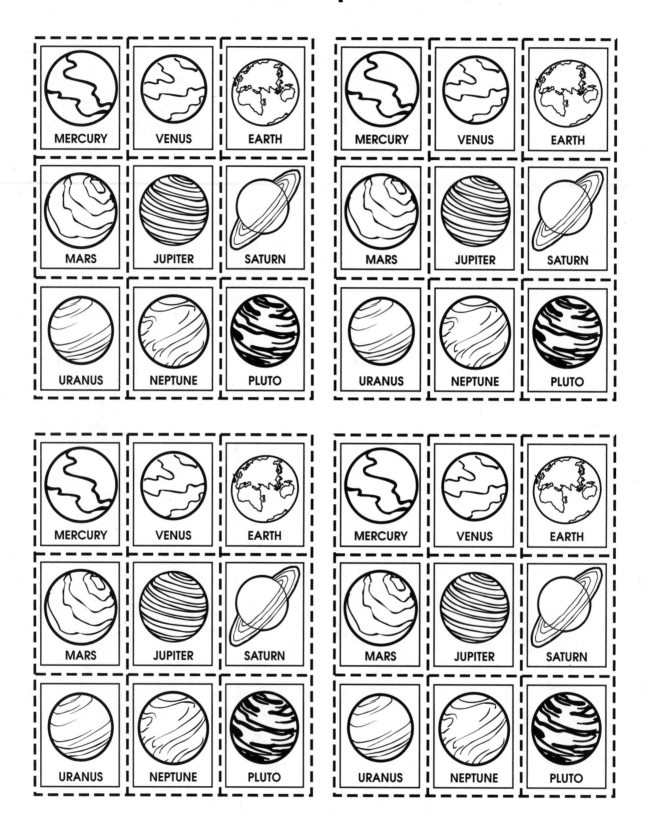

The Magic Rocket

Story:

The Magic Rocket by Steven Kroll, illustrated by Will Hillenbrand (Holiday House, 1992).

In this story, a little boy named Felix gets a toy rocket for his birthday. It's long and thin and gold, has three booster engines and a shiny cockpit, and glows when Felix looks at it. Felix embarks on a space journey that takes him into contact with aliens when he rescues his pet dog Atom.

Setting the Stage:

- Give children drawing paper and markers or crayons to create creatures from other planets. Post these on a "Creature Feature" bulletin board.
- Let children make their own magic rockets from toilet paper tubes, colored cellophane, glue, glitter, and tempera paint. Display on a table, or thread through with yarn and hang from a clothesline strung across the classroom.
- Set out photo books of rockets and other space crafts (see "Nonfiction Resources" for suggestions).

Tricky Tongue Twister:

Rockets dock in rocket dockers.

Magic Rocket Rides

Materials:
Writing paper, pencils, drawing paper, crayons or markers, additional art supplies (gold or aluminum foil, glitter, glue, star stickers, reinforcements—which make great portholes!)

Directions:
1. Have your students imagine that they went on their own ride through space in a magic rocket, chasing after space creatures to rescue a pet (either real or imaginary).
2. Provide writing paper and pencils for students to record what happened on their journeys. You can give them writing prompts, for example:
   - What did your rocket look like?
   - Were you scared to ride in space?
   - What was the best part of the ride?
   - How did you rescue your pet?
3. Children can illustrate their stories with pictures. Provide art materials for them to use to draw their rockets.
4. Post the completed stories and pictures, or bind them in a classroom book.

2095

Story:

2095 by Jon Scieszka, illustrated by Lane Smith (Viking, 1995).
2095 tells of the adventures of a group of youngsters, known as the "Time Warp Trio." This chapter book describes what happens when they arrive in a very futuristic New York City.

Setting the Stage:

- Bring old calendars into the classroom and post the pages around the room.
- Use the refrigerator-box rocket from the Hands-on Discoveries "Super-Duper Project" (p. 22) as a time-traveling machine.
- Have children draw pictures of what they think they'll look like in 10, 20, or 30 years.
- Ask children to bring in baby pictures. Post these on a bulletin board with current class pictures. Have the children observe the amount of change that can occur in only a couple of years.

Tricky Tongue Twister:

Make a planetary plan for no pollution.

Lesson for the Future

Materials:
Drawing paper, crayons or markers

Directions:
1. Have the children imagine that they are time travelers, visiting from the future.
2. Divide the class into two groups, one group that comes from a sad future where the planet is filled with pollution and the other that comes from a happier, cleaner future.
3. Discuss the fact that in order to keep our Earth healthy in the future, people need to take care of it today.
4. Have children draw pictures of two possible future worlds, one with pollution, litter, etc., and the other clean.
5. Have children brainstorm "positive Earth" slogans, for example, "Keep Earth clean today for a brighter tomorrow."
6. Post the pictures around the school, along with signs with the slogans. Make sure that the signs are posted in areas where people have a tendency to litter: lunchrooms, playgrounds, bike racks, and so on.

Option:
Get other classes involved in a school-wide pollution/litter awareness project.

Milky Way Journal

In *Postcards from Pluto*, the travelers visit the different planets. In *2095*, the "Time Warp Trio" goes to the future. Felix, in *The Magic Rocket*, whisks through space to find his dog. In this activity, children will venture (in their minds) to the planet, star, or other space "object" of their choice and write a journal or log about their experience.

Materials:
"A to Z Space List" (p. 78), "Super-Duper Fact Cards" (pp. 70-77), "Milky Way Journal" Hands-on Handouts (pp. 60-61), pencils, crayons or markers

Directions:
1. Duplicate the "A to Z Space List" and let children choose a location they would like to visit.
2. Duplicate the "Milky Way Journal" Hands-on Handouts for each child to use as a prompt. The children can continue their journals on additional pieces of paper if they wish. They can illustrate their journals with crayons or markers.
3. Children can set their stories in the past, present, or future.
4. Have the children write a journal entry based on facts they've learned about their chosen location. (They can brush up on these facts by using the "Super-Duper Fact Cards.") The entries will be a mixture of fact and fiction (like the *Postcards from Pluto* book). Children will not really visit the planet, but they can use facts they've learned to create an interesting story.
5. Once the stories are completed, let the children read them to the class.

Option:
Invite other classes in to hear your students' journal stories.

Milky Way Journal

Date_____

Name _____

I traveled in a _____

I visited _____

I saw_____

The temperature was _____

I met_____

I will never forget _____

_____

_____

_____

_____

_____

_____

Milky Way Journal

I saw_____ on my visit.

It looked like

Spectactular Space Program

Songs:
- A Black Hole Is Just Like a Vacuum
- Ring-a-Ring 'Round Saturn
- I See a Bright Star
- Asteroid Rock
- My Planet's Number Three
- I'm Where I Want to Be
- Nebulas Are Clouds of Dust
- Twinkle, Twinkle,
- Take Me Up in a Spaceship
- Our Sun Is a Star

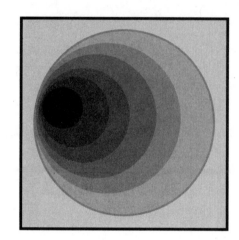

Featuring:

A Black Hole Is Just Like a Vacuum

(to the tune of "My Bonnie Lies Over the Ocean")

A black hole is just like a vacuum,
It sucks things right out of the sky.
Its gravity pulls with a power
On neighboring stars way up high
   (up high).

Black hole, oh, black hole,
Don't try out your vacuum on me, on me.
Black hole, oh, black hole,
Don't try out your vacuum on me.

Ring-a-Ring 'Round Saturn

(to the tune of "Ring-a-Ring O' Roses")

Ring-a-ring 'round Saturn.
The rings are in a pattern.
Ice and rocks go 'round and round.

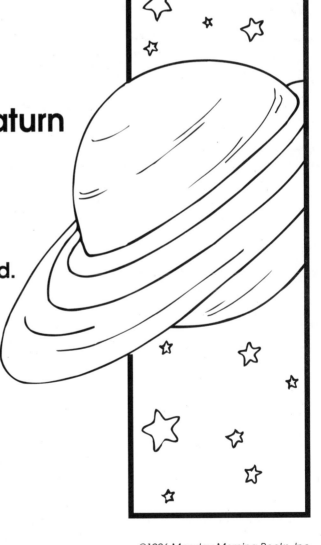

I See a Bright Star

(to the tune of "You Are My Sunshine")

I see a bright star,
It's not a night star.
It only shines bright
During the day.
Right through my window
It casts a warm glow,
A lovely sunbeam, a bright golden ray.

When other stars shine,
Yes, when it's nighttime,
This single star sets off in the west.
It goes to bring light
Where others have night,
Because our star, called "the sun,"
Never rests.

Asteroid Rock

(to the tune of "Jingle Bell Rock")

Asteroid, asteroid, asteroid rock,
Asteroids orbit through asteroid space.
These tiny planets collide in the air,
Spaceships, be aware!

Asteroid, asteroid, asteroid rock,
Ceres is largest, and Hathor is small.
Vesta's the brightest, it shines in the night,
What an awesome sight.

When you're traveling in a spaceship,
Better open your eyes.
For an asteroid can be dangerous,
It can knock you out of the sky!

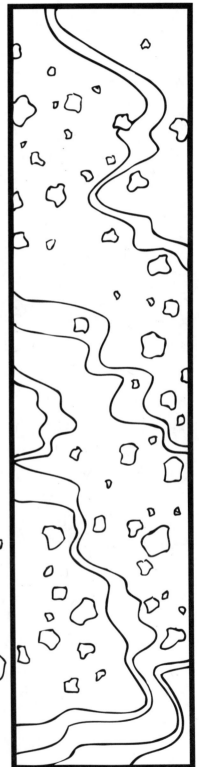

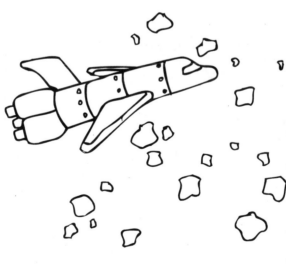

My Planet's Number Three

(to the tune of "My Country 'Tis of Thee")

My planet's number three,
Two after Mercury,
Earth is my home.
Venus is much too hot,
Jupiter's not the spot,
Neptune and Pluto, I think not.
I will never roam.

I'm Where I Want to Be

(to the tune of "My Country 'Tis of Thee")

I'm where I want to be
Thanks to Earth's gravity,
I can be sure.
Earth's where I want to play,
I will not fly away,
'Cause gravity makes sure I'll stay
Firmly on the floor.

Nebulas Are Clouds of Dust

(to the tune of "London Bridges")

Nebulas are clouds of dust,
Gas and dust,
Gas and dust.
Nebulas are clouds of dust,
Stars are born here.

Twinkle, Twinkle

(to the tune of "Twinkle, Twinkle, Little Star")

Twinkle, twinkle, little star,
How I wonder what you are.
Gas and dust clouds
Pulled in tight.
Heat that shines with all its might.
Dust and gas around a core,
Twinkle just a little more.

Take Me Up in a Spaceship

(to the tune of "Take Me Out to the Ball Game")

Take me up in a spaceship,
Take me right to the moon.
I want to visit a distant place,
I want to go into outer space.

Oh, the Earth looks small
From the moon's crust,
It's only a ball shining bright.
But it glows with light all its own
In the dark, black night.

Our Sun Is a Star

(to the tune of "Home On the Range")

Our sun is a star.
It is not very far
From the Earth—
Which is why it's so bright.
It's medium-hot, which is still quite a lot,
So, don't look at it right in the light.

Each bright sunny day,
I make sure when I go out to play,
That I wear a hat,
And a parasol that
Will protect me from sun's harmful rays.

Black Hole Facts

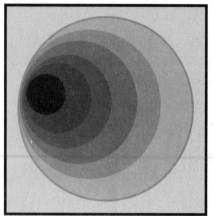

What it is: The brightest stars in the universe turn into black holes when they die.

How it happens: When a large star dies, gravity pulls its gases toward the center. The gases pack closer together and become a black hole.

Name game: No light can escape from a black hole.

Super-Duper Fact: X-rays help tell us there are black holes.

Comet Facts

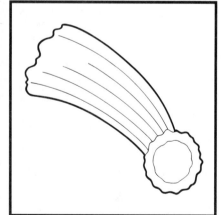

What it is: A comet is a frozen mixture of ice, dust, and rock.

What it looks like: Comets look like giant "dirty snowballs" moving through space.

The comet's tail: The tail is made when the comet passes near the sun. Gas and dust bits stretch back, away from the sun, to form a long glowing tail.

Super-Duper Fact: Comet tails may be millions of miles long. However, there is not enough material in them to fill a large suitcase.

Earth Facts

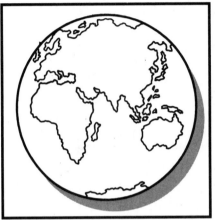

Size: Earth's size is right in the middle of the nine planets. There are four planets smaller than Earth, and four planets larger.
It moves: Earth moves in two ways. It spins, and it also travels around the sun. The path it takes around the sun is almost a perfect circle.
Color: From space, Earth looks blue.

Super-Duper Fact: Water covers three-quarters of the Earth's surface. Earth is the only planet that has water.

Jupiter Facts

Size: Jupiter is the biggest planet. It is about 63 times bigger than Pluto.
Description: From Earth, Jupiter looks like a bright star in the sky.
Color: Jupiter looks silver-white.
Moons: Jupiter has 16 moons.
Name: Jupiter was named for the king of the gods of ancient Rome.

Super-Duper Fact: Jupiter is larger than the other eight planets put together.

Mars Facts

Size: Mars is the third smallest planet.

Color: Mars is called the "red planet" because it is covered in red dust. Even the sky is red on Mars.

Two moons: Mars has two tiny moons named Phobos and Deimos.

Temperature: It is very cold on Mars.

Super-Duper Fact: Mars has dust storms that can last for weeks. Strong winds pick up the red dust and move it about the surface.

Mercury Facts

Size: Mercury is the second smallest planet.

No moon: Mercury doesn't have a moon.

No gas: Mercury is almost airless. It has no atmosphere (no layer of gas around it).

Hot/cold: Mercury is very hot during the day. It is very cold at night.

Super-Duper Fact: Mercury is covered with bowl-shaped hollows called craters. The craters will never wear away because there is no wind or water on Mercury.

Moon Facts

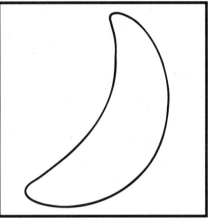

Craters: The moon's craters were made by space rocks that crashed into it thousands of millions of years ago.
Moon-walkers: Earth and the moon are the only places on which humans have walked. Twelve men have been to the moon.
No air: There is no air to breathe on the Moon.

Super-Duper Fact: Eighty-one Earth moons together would weigh the same as Earth.

Neptune Facts

Size: Neptune is the fourth largest planet. It is slightly smaller than Uranus.
Color: Neptune is blue-green. It has dark and light spots on its surface.
Dim ring: Neptune has rings, but they are very dim.
Moons (or satellites): Neptune has eight satellites.

Super-Duper Fact: Neptune has the most wind of all the planets.

Pluto Facts

Size: Pluto is the smallest planet. It is smaller than Earth's moon.
Location: Pluto is the farthest planet from the sun. From Pluto, the sun looks like a bright star.
Temperature: Pluto is very cold. It hardly gets any heat or light from the sun.
Moon: Pluto has one known moon. It is called Charon.

Super-Duper Fact: Pluto has the longest year. It lasts 248 Earth years.

Red Giant Facts

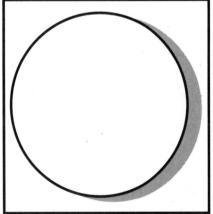

Color: Red giants are stars that have used up all their hydrogen. Their surface cools and turns red.
What happens: When the surface of the star cools, it swells up and becomes a "giant."
Next step: After the red giant uses all its fuel, it shrinks and becomes a white dwarf.

Super-Duper Fact: The sun won't become a red giant for another five billion years.

Saturn Facts

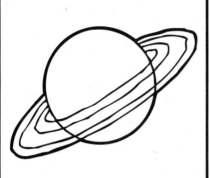

Size: Saturn is the second largest planet.
Many moons: At least 18 moons orbit Saturn.
Rings: Saturn's rings are made of millions of pieces of rock and ice.
Fast day: Saturn's day (the time it takes to spin around once) is 10 hours and 14 minutes long.

Super-Duper Fact: Saturn's rings are huge but very thin.

Star Facts

Size: The biggest stars are much bigger than the sun, and the smallest stars are much smaller than Earth.
Color: All stars are very hot, but some are hotter than others. Blue-white stars are the hottest of all. Yellow-orange ones are cooler. Red stars are coolest.
Age: Stars live for millions of years.

Super-Duper Fact: Even red stars are 20 times hotter than the heat from a kitchen oven!

Sun Facts

Day star: The sun is a star.
Size: The sun is only a medium-sized star. Other stars are much larger.
Off-color: The sun has some blotches called sunspots.
Weather: Sunspots may cause changes in the Earth's weather.

Super-Duper Fact: A million Earths could be squashed inside of the sun.

Uranus Facts

Size: Uranus is the third largest planet.
Tilted: Uranus spins on its side as it orbits the sun.
Ring: Uranus has a ring made of 13 separate rings of dark rock.
Satellites (or moons): Uranus has 15 satellites altogether. The five main ones are Miranda, Ariel, Umbriel, Titanio, and Oberon.

Super-Duper Fact: Uranus's small satellite, Miranda, may have crashed together with another body. It seems to have broken into large pieces that came together again.

Venus Facts

Size: Venus is the fourth smallest planet.
Cloudy days: Venus is surrounded by a thick layer of clouds.
Temperature: Venus is very hot.
Poison: The gas in Venus's clouds are poisonous.
Name: Venus is named after the goddess of love.

Super-Duper Fact: Venus shines more brightly than any other planet.

White Dwarf Facts

First a giant: As a star grows old, its core becomes hotter and swells up. The star becomes a red giant.
What happens: When a red giant becomes a white dwarf, all the material packs close together.
Temperature: A white dwarf is a small but very hot star.
The end: Finally, the white dwarf cools and fades away.

Super-Duper Fact: In time, the sun will cool and shrink. It will become a white dwarf about the size of Earth.

Space A to Z List

A: Asteroids, Astronauts, Atmosphere
B: Black Hole
C: Comet, Corona
D: Deimos, Dog Star
E: Earth, Eclipse, Evening Star
F: Fornax Dwarf, Freedom Space Station
G: Gravity, Great Comet
H: Halley's Comet
I: Ice, Io
J: Jupiter
K: Kepler's Star
L: Launches, Lunar Probes, Lunar Eclipses
M: Mars, Mercury, Meteor, Milky Way, Moon
N: Neptune, North Star
O: Orion, Oxygen
P: Planets, Pluto
Q: Quasar
R: Rings
S: Satellites, Shooting Star, Solar System, Sun
T: Titan
U: Universe, Uranus
V: Vacuum, Venus, Volcanoes
W: White Dwarfs
X: X-ray Telescopes
Z: Zodiac Signs

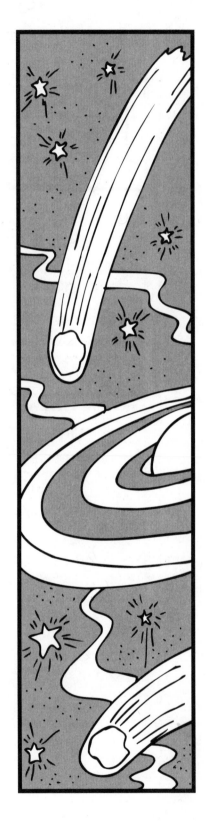

Nonfiction Resources

- *Americans to the Moon* by Gene Gurney (Random House, 1970).
- *An Album of Voyager* by Maury Solomon (Franklin Watts, 1990).
- *Aurora: The Mysterious Northern Lights* by Candace Sherk Savage (Sierra Club Books, 1994).
- *The Aurora Watchers Handbook* by Neil T. Davis (University of Alaska Press, 1992).
- *The Big Dipper and You* by E.C. Krupp (Morrow Junior Books, 1989).
- *A Book of Stars for You* by Franklyn M. Branley, illustrated by Leonard Kessler (Crowell, 1967).
- *The Comet and You* by E. C. Krupp (Macmillan, 1985).
- *Comets* by Martyn Hamer (Franklin Watts, 1984).
- *Comets, Meteors, and Asteroids* by Seymour Simon (Morrow Junior Books, 1994).
- *The Creation of the Universe* by David E. Fisher (The Bobbs-Merrill Company, 1977).
- *The Day We Walked on the Moon: A Photo History of Space Exploration* by George Sullivan (Scholastic, 1990).
- *Exploring the Sun* by Roy A. Gallant (Garden City Books, 1958).
- *Find the Constellations* by H. A. Rey, revised edition (Houghton Mifflin, 1976).
- *The Glow-in-the-Dark Zodiac* by Katherine Ross, illustrated by Stephen Marchesi (Random House, 1993).
- *The History of Manned Space Flight* by David Baker (Crown, 1982).
- *I Want to Know About a Flight to the Moon* by Alfred M. Worden with introduction by Fred Rogers (Doubleday, 1974).
- *Journey into a Black Hole* by Franklyn M. Branley (Crowell, 1986).
- *Journey to the Planets* by Patricia Lauber (Crown, 1990).
- *Jupiter* by Seymour Simon (William Morrow, 1985).
- *Jupiter: The Spotted Giant* by Isaac Asimov (Gareth Stevens, 1989).

©1996 *Monday Morning Books, Inc.*

- *Let's Go to the Moon* by Michael Chester (Putnam, 1974).
- *Let's Go to the Moon* by Janis Knudsen Wheat (National Geographic Society, 1977).
- *The Long View into Space* by Seymour Simon (Crown, 1979).
- *Mars* by Elaine Landau (Franklin Watts, 1991).
- *Mercury* by Seymour Simon (Morrow Junior Books, 1992).
- *Mysteries of the Planets* by Franklyn M. Branley (E. P. Dutton, 1988).
- *Night Sky* by Carole Stott (Dorling Kindersley, 1993).
- *Northern Lights* by Dorothy M. Souza (Carolrhoda Books, 1994).
- *One Giant Leap* by Mary Ann Fraser (Holt, 1993).
- *1000 Facts About Space* by Pam Beasant (Kingfisher, 1992).
- *Our Solar System* by Seymour Simon (Morrow Junior Books, 1992).
- *The Picture World of Rockets and Satellites* by Norman S. Barrett (Franklyn Watts, 1990).
- *Pieces of Another World: The Story of Moon Rocks* by Franklyn M. Branley (Crowell, 1972).
- *Rockets and Satellites* by Franklyn M. Branley (Harper & Row, 1987).
- *Saturn* by Seymour Simon (William Morrow, 1985).
- *Saturn: The Ringed Beauty* by Isaac Asimov (Gareth Stevens, 1989).
- *Space Scientist: The Sun* by Heather Couper and Nigel Henbest (Franklin Watts, 1986).
- *Stargazers* by Gail Gibbons (Holiday House, 1992).
- *Stars* by Michael George (Creative Education, 1991).
- *Stars* by Seymour Simon (William Morris, 1986).
- *The Third Planet: Exploring the Earth from Space* by Sally Ride and Tam O'Shaughnessy (Crown, 1994).
- *The True Story of the Moon-ride Rock Hunt* by Margaret Friskey (Childrens Press, 1972).
- *The Universe* by Herbert S. Zim (William Morrow, 1973).
- *Uranus* by Seymour Simon (William Morrow, 1987).
- *Venus* by Seymour Simon (Morrow Junior Books, 1992).